Puppy Training

How To Stop Your Puppy From Peeing Indoors And Raise The Perfect Dog In 7 Days Without Accidents

-- *By* Toni Tomson --

Copyright © 2020 by Toni Tomson

ISBN: 9798623710802

All rights reserved. No part of this guide may be reproduced in any form without permission in writing from the publisher, except for brief quotations used for publishable articles or reviews.

Legal Disclaimer

The information contained in this book and its contents is not designed to replace any form of medical or professional advice; and is not meant to replace the need for independent medical, financial, legal, or other professional advice or services that may be required. The content and information in this book have been provided for educational and entertainment purposes only.

The content and information contained in this book have been compiled from sources deemed reliable, and they are accurate to the best of the Author's knowledge, information, and belief. However, the Author cannot guarantee its accuracy and validity and therefore cannot be held liable for any errors and/or omissions. Further, changes are periodically made to this book as needed. Where appropriate and/or necessary, you must consult a professional (including but not limited to your doctor, attorney, financial advisor, or other such professional) before using any of the suggested remedies, techniques, and/or information in this book.

Upon using this book's contents and information, you agree to hold harmless the Author from any damages, costs, and expenses, including any legal fees, potentially resulting from the application of any of the information in this book. This disclaimer applies to any loss, damages, or injury caused by the use and application of this book's contents, whether directly or indirectly, whether for breach of contract, tort, negligence, personal injury, criminal intent, or under any other circumstance.

You agree to accept all risks of using the information presented in this book.

You agree that by continuing to read this book, where appropriate and/or necessary, you shall consult a professional (including but not limited to your doctor, attorney, financial advisor, or other such professional) before using any of the suggested remedies, techniques, or information in this book.

Table of Contents

One Introduction 1
Two Learning The Basics 3
Three Keep Your Puppy Close 11
Four Timeline And Tips 16
Five Setting A Training Routine 22
Six Creating An Area 27
Seven How To Prevent Accidents 32
Eight Puppy Potty Training Mistakes 36
Frequently asked questions 44
Conclusion 49

One
Introduction

One of the main reasons why puppies and dogs end up in shelters is because the owners are not successful at training them. Having said that, you cannot expect to train your puppy fully before he is six months old. You can, however, begin the training when your puppy is at least two weeks old. Your puppy needs to know that he cannot relieve himself anywhere around the house. You must train your puppy since this will help to strengthen your bond with him.

When your puppy is only a few weeks old, he will not have sufficient bowel and bladder control. This means that you need to be vigilant during that period because he just cannot hold it in. You cannot, however, start training him the moment he sets foot inside your home. Bear in mind that there will be a handful of accidents. But do not fret. This book will tell you all you need to know about how to deal with such mishaps.

Some owners are under the misconception that it is easy to train their puppies. They think that maintaining a routine will help them train the puppy easily. Or they believe that their puppy will be housetrained in just two weeks. This may work for some puppies, but many puppies who are taken through such a shortened and easygoing potty training will only be half-trained. These puppies will continue to have these mishaps for months. Puppies will understand that it is good for them to go potty outdoors, but they do not understand that they cannot go indoors.

Through potty training, you need to teach your puppy where it is that he can go. But you also need to let him know where it is that he cannot go. This book will help you learn what you need to do to potty train your puppy.

Two
Learning The Basics

When you bring your puppy into a new home, you need to ensure that you stay calm and patient. Your puppy is in a new environment, and he will have accidents. You need to bear this in mind when you train your puppy. This chapter will shed some light on the basics you need to bear in mind.

Introduce your Puppy to your Home

You must introduce your puppy to your home. You need to introduce him to his new role and family. Your puppy is going to be excited about the new house. He may also be bursting with curiosity, fear, joy, and excitement. It is a good time to lay the foundation now with your pet. Give your puppy enough time to learn to respect and trust you and his new family. This is the only way you can set the right expectations with your puppy. You also need to make sure that you are consistent with them.

You should show your puppy the areas where he can be. You should never let your pet explore the area on his own, especially if you do not want to let them poop or pee in the area. For instance, if you do not want your puppy to go to your bedroom or other areas in the house, you cannot allow your puppy to walk towards those areas.

Understand the Needs of your Puppy

You need to understand your puppy's breed. Make sure that you understand the behavior and are aware of it. For example, if you have a Shitzsu at home, you know that these puppies have small bladders. They will need to urinate more often, and there will be some accidents even if you train them well. Dogs are very intelligent, but they do not think of the way human beings do. You cannot expect your puppy to tell you when they need to poop or pee. Therefore, you need to understand how they communicate and look for clues.

Be Watchful

Make sure your puppy is always where you can see him when you are training him. When you can see him, you can look for signs or signals that your puppy is giving you, so you know he needs to go. This will help you prevent accidents from happening. Some signs that they may give you are scratching, sniffing, and circling. Some puppies may also whine or bark. If you see these signs, take him to the spot where you want him to pee or poop and let him ease himself.

Interrupt Accidents

If your puppy pees or poops inside the house, you need to make a sudden noise to tell him to stop. You can also use a command to do this as it will remind him that he needs to go outside to relieve himself. Keep the following points in mind when you do this:

- You do not want to scare your puppy, but only want to startle him. Your intention should only be to gain his attention, so you can let him know that you do not want him to pee or poop indoors. Remain consistent – this means you need to use the same action or word every time.

- If he is pooping indoors, you cannot stop him immediately because he will not be able to stop this. You should still use the same action or command, so he knows what he is doing is wrong.

- Do not punish your puppy when there are accidents. The little one does not know right from wrong.

You should not remind them constantly about their actions. If you are aggressive, they will be scared of you.

- You should never use punishment during potty training. This will either confuse the puppy or lead to more accidents. If your puppy sees that you are mad when he poops or pees, he will be scared of you. He will not tell you when he needs to go and will most likely poop or pee in places that you cannot reach.

Find A Spot

You must choose a spot where it is okay for your puppy to pee or poop. Make sure that other dogs do not visit this spot, and it is easy for you to clean. We will look at this in further detail later in the book, but keep the following points in mind:

- When your puppy smells the urine, he will associate that spot as his bathroom.

- You need to choose an easily accessible area. Remember that you will visit this area quite often when you train your puppy.

- Do not choose spots where other dogs come until your puppy has been given all the rounds of vaccine. You can discuss this further with your vet.

- When you take your puppy outside, keep him on a leash. This way, you can teach him to go in a specific location. You can also keep an eye on him to know when he is done.

Choose a Command or Word

As mentioned earlier, you should stop your puppy from peeing or pooping inside the house using an action or command. You should also use a command to indicate to them when they need to go. Use this command when you take your puppy outside to relieve himself. This will also help him understand that he needs only to use that spot to relieve himself. Your puppy will soon recognize the command and will know what he needs to do. Do not use this command to indicate anything else. Otherwise, you can confuse the puppy.

Appreciate your Puppy

When your puppy learns to pee or poop in the right area, you should praise him. Make sure to use a happy and cheerful voice to let him know that you are pleased. Always be consistent with how you show emotion.

Make the Process Relaxing

Your puppy should associate peeing and pooping as a rewarding activity. You should encourage your puppy to be patient while he controls himself until he reaches his area. You can set a routine. Your puppy should enjoy going for a walk and relieving himself. You should never interrupt or hurry your puppy when he is relieving himself. Let him relax and take his time.

Always Clean Up

Your puppy is bound to have accidents inside the house. You need to clean the area immediately and thoroughly. This will tell your puppy that he should not relieve himself in the same place.

Three
Keep Your Puppy Close

When you are training your puppy, you need to keep an eye on him. You will know when he needs to relieve himself based on some signs or signals.

Limit the Area

One of the easiest ways to keep your puppy close to you is to limit the areas where he can roam about freely. You can use baby gates or close the doors so he knows where he should not go. When your puppy is restricted to a smaller area, you can observe him and know when he needs to go out. Make sure that the area is large enough so he can play and roam about freely. You can use a small room or an area that you have closed off using gates. Make sure that you choose an area that is very close to the outdoors and is easy to clean. Remember that your puppy will have accidents at the start, and you need to ensure that you put him in an area that is easy to clean. You can use a crate if you want to limit the number of accidents. When you train your puppy correctly using a crate, you can ensure that your puppy will not relieve himself inside the crate when you are not there to clean. You will also teach your puppy to control his bladder. This will enhance the process and make it easier for both you and your puppy.

Use a Short Leash

When you keep your puppy on a leash, you can move freely around the house and also keep an eye on your puppy. You can move from one room to the next and still keep your puppy next to you. You can ensure that you always see where your puppy is. You should only do this when you know you cannot give your puppy your undivided attention. This way, when your puppy has an accident, you can always clean up quickly and encourage him to go inside.

Crate Training

As mentioned earlier, it is a good idea to use a crate to train your puppy. If you cannot watch your dog continuously, you should use a crate. There will be times when you need to leave the house, maybe for work, and it is a good idea to use a crate. When you teach your puppy to live inside the crate, he will think of the crate as his home. He will learn not to soil the area because he has to live inside it. Here are some points you need to bear in mind when you do this:

- Make sure the crate is large enough for your puppy. You need to buy a crate that will be big enough for him as he grows older. The crate should be big enough for him to sleep in or turn around. Do not buy a very big crate because your puppy may use the other end as the bathroom.

- You can buy a large crate when you bring a puppy home, but make sure that you block the extra space. The crate will be the right size for the puppy.

- You must ensure that your puppy loves spending time in the crate; leave a few treats and toys in there to encourage him to go in and stay in.

- Do not let your puppy spend too long inside the crate. Limit the time he spends in the crate to less than an hour at one time. Remember, he has a small bladder and cannot control himself. So, let him out of the crate as often as possible so that he can relieve himself.

- Puppies as young as a few days can only hold their urine for an hour. So, never leave your puppy inside the crate for longer than an hour.

- When you take your puppy out of the crate, you should take him for a walk. Until your puppy is fully potty trained, you should not leave him inside the crate for too long. You need to keep an eye on him to limit the mess he will make.

Four
Timeline And Tips

You need to teach your puppy never to make a mess inside the house. You can fully train your puppy in seven days if you establish a timeline and stick to it. When you adhere to this timeline, it should include information about where your puppy can and cannot relieve himself. As mentioned earlier, you can use crates or even puppy pads to make your training more effective.

In the Morning

Your puppy needs consistency. This means that your days should start the same every day. When your alarm goes off, you need to get out of bed and take your puppy out for a walk so he can finish his business. Do not wait to drink coffee or check your phone for any notifications. Try to keep the crate or puppy pad near the bathroom or close to your room. When you hear your puppy whine in the night, you can take your puppy out so he can relieve himself. When your puppy is small, you can pick him up and carry him outside. This will let him know that he should not pee outside the crate or anywhere on the floor in the house.

Make sure that you always walk out of the same door to the same spot where you want your puppy to pee or poop. As mentioned earlier, you can keep him on a leash, so you know when he wants to go.

After Food

You need to take him out for a walk after every meal. This is another thing you can do in the morning. The minute you are done with breakfast, walk out of the door with him. Make sure that you always stick to the schedule. You can slowly regulate your puppy's bowel movements in this way. Do not wait for too long after you finish a meal to take him out for a walk. You can give yourself a gap of 5 – 30 minutes after any meal before you go out. When your puppy is younger, you need to be faster. Make sure that you take your puppy out immediately after a meal. As your puppy grows older, he will learn to control himself. Puppies eat almost four meals every day, and they definitely need to poop after their meal. So, you need to pay attention to this period. You need to be careful about how much water your puppy drinks. You need to consider this also a meal and take him out to poop or pee

After Naps and Playtime

Puppies will also need to go out at other times. They may need to go after playtime and naps. Their naps will be a smaller version of your morning routine. You must take your puppy out for a walk immediately after they wake up from a nap. When your puppy is playing, his digestive system will be stimulated. This will make him want to poop. Make sure that you understand the signals and lead your puppy away from the house to his spot. Some signs you need to be aware of are:

- Scratching or sniffing the floor
- Walking away from family
- Whining
- Pawing

Praise

As you and your puppy establish a routine, you need to pay attention to what you are doing outside. As mentioned earlier, you need to find a spot that will become your puppy's spot. We will look at how you should choose the area later in the book. Make sure to use a command or sound to indicate to him that he can do his business in that spot. You should also appreciate him for easing himself in the right spot. You need to do this every time you are outside. When you do this, your puppy will understand that he will receive a lot of treats when he does his business in the right spot.

If your puppy does not like pooping or peeing in front of you, you may need to head in for a few minutes and then head back out. You may also need to take him out a few minutes after he is done. So, stay vigilant. As mentioned earlier, you should not punish your puppy if he has accidents inside the house. Remember to use a command or sound to stop him. If you want, you can also place a bell on the door. Teach your puppy to ring the bell when he needs to pee or poop. This way, you will know when you need to go outside. When you walk your puppy outside to do his business, ring the bell with your hand. Do this until your puppy learns to ring the bell when he needs to go out. As soon as your puppy learns to do this, praise him.

Last Call

If you need to leave home for a long time, maybe to go to the office or out for dinner, you need to plan ahead. If you do not know how long you will be away from home, you should use the month-plus-one rule. This rule will help you calculate the number of hours you can leave your puppy alone for between potty breaks. Calculate the month of your puppy in months and add one to it. This is the total number of hours you can leave your puppy alone for. If you have a two-month-old puppy, you can leave him alone for three hours with the certainty that he will not create a mess. Remember to take your puppy for one last break before you all go to bed. Your puppy cannot hold on to her bladder for a long time.

You cannot expect to succeed in training your puppy overnight. It will take some time to set a routine. So, you need to be patient. We will look at some tips in the next chapter to help you set a routine.

Five
Setting A Training Routine

Puppies are happy creatures, but when you are training your puppy, you need to make sure that you have a routine that will allow them to feel secure. When you build a routine and create rules in the house, you will let the baby know what he needs to expect. You need to ensure that every person in your house also sticks to the routine. What you need to remember is that you are bringing a puppy out of an environment he knows to a new place. The little one has left his mother and friends, traveled in a car, and entered a house that has unfamiliar people, sounds, and smells. There can be other animals in the house who are new to them too. This will make the puppy lose confidence. When you establish a schedule, your puppy will know what to expect. It will also reduce any stress that the little one is feeling.

Define the Rules

When you set the rules, you need to let everybody at home know the rules too. You can set these rules before the puppy comes home, but you can do it after you bring him home too. He will be confused if one of you allows him to enter the bedroom, and one of you does not. Every puppy needs consistency during training. You cannot change the rules for them during training because that will confuse them. This confusion will strain your relationship with him. You must decide the following before you begin training:

- Is he allowed on the furniture?

- Can he sleep in your room?

- Will he sleep inside a crate, on a pillow, or in the garage?

You need to decide fast. You can allow him to sleep in the same room since that will help you bond quickly. The key is to ensure that the entire family is on board with the rules.

Potty Routine

When you stick to a routine, your puppy will learn better and faster. You need to choose a location that is easily accessible and one that can be cleaned easily. We will discuss how you need to choose a spot in the next chapter. Make sure the entire family knows where he is allowed to go. If you constantly change the spot, your pet will be confused. When you stick to one area, your puppy knows where he needs to go by the scent. As mentioned earlier, you need to schedule a potty break. Remember, you can tweak the potty schedule a little as he grows older. However, you need to stick to the schedule in the beginning. This will improve the process and prevent any accidents.

Meals

You need to schedule your puppy's meals, too. You also must choose a specific location where your puppy is allowed to eat. You need to decide if you want to give him treats during lunch or whatever food is on the table. You can give him healthy treats if you like, but do not give them treats right before a meal. This will spoil his appetite. Since you cannot give the puppy most of the food that you eat, do not let him watch you snacking in the evening. You should never expect the puppy to only eat from his bowl. You can compromise and let him eat from a bowl that is placed on the table too. You can fill that bowl with some food from the table and offer that to the little one as food or dessert.

Exercise

You may have heard people tell you that a puppy is well behaved when he is tired. If your puppy is energetic, you may need to spend a lot of time playing with him during the day. Make sure to give him a lot of exercise, so he gets tired. Puppies play for many reasons. When you play with your puppy, you can bond with him. Make sure to use these parts of the day to teach him something new. You can spend five minutes every day teaching him something new and reminding him of earlier lessons. You need to wear him out, so he sleeps enough.

Six
Creating An Area

Your puppy will make a mess of the yard and your house. They think they can relieve themselves wherever they find a place. Your lawn will look less attractive when your puppy pees everywhere because the pee will leave some brown spots on your grass. You may also miss scooping some poop and step on it later. It is also not very sanitary or appealing if you need to spend a lot of time in your yard trying to clean the mess up. However, you can teach your dog how to stick to a designated area in the yard.

Choose the Right Spot

You need to choose a spot in your yard that is not in everybody's sight. This spot should be where your puppy will poop or pee every day. Remember, you need to find a spot that will be appropriate as your puppy grows, too. You can choose a small area if you have a small breed, but a larger breed will need more area. You also need to find a space that will not become too dirty and smelly. You can also let your puppy choose a spot for himself. If your puppy returns to only one area to relieve himself, let that become his toilet area. You need to ensure that you choose a spot that is realistic for both you and your puppy.

Clean the Area

You always need to keep the toilet area clean. You keep your bathroom clean, don't you? The same goes for your puppy's area. You can leave a little pile in the spot, so your puppy knows that he needs to go there to poop or pee. You should never leave too much poop there since it will smell. He will choose another spot to relieve himself if the area smells terrible.

Train on Command

One of the best ways to train your puppy to use only one spot is to use a command. This has been mentioned earlier in the book. What you need to do here is to take your puppy on a leash and walk towards the spot. You should then use a command that will let him know that he needs to pee or poop only in that spot. Make sure to reward your puppy if he relieves himself in the right spot.

Stick to One Spot

You will not let the puppy run around the house until he is house trained. The same goes for your yard too. You should ensure that you train your puppy to stick to only one spot in your yard. One of the best ways to do this is to take him to the yard on a leash and stand in the same spot until your puppy goes. You should never let him explore the yard. If you want, you can use temporary fencing to block the area. Make sure that you leave your puppy in that area, and give him the cue. Let your dog out of the enclosure only when he is done with his business.

Reward

This has not been said enough. You need to reward your puppy every time he goes in the right spot. But you should not let your puppy run around the yard if he did not go yet. Your dog may not always want to go when you take him out. If that is the case, you should take him back inside the house and try again.

Proofing Behavior

When your puppy continues to go to the right spot to poop, you should make sure that you clean it up immediately. Rinse the urine using a hose and scoop the poop. If your puppy does not stick to the right spot, do not hit or scold him. You should take him inside immediately and not praise him. When he does not receive praise, he knows that he made a mistake. He will learn quickly that he needs to only poop or pee in the right spot. You can see if your puppy has learned to do this when you are not at home. If you take your puppy out with you to a friend's house, for instance, ask the owner where they would prefer their puppy pees or poops. Take your puppy to the spot, hold him on the leash, use the command, and wait. If your puppy goes in that spot, you know your training has worked. You need to make sure you clean up after your dog no matter where he pees or poops.

Seven
How To Prevent Accidents

Puppies are bound to have accidents. Puppy potty training accidents are often unavoidable, especially in the first few days or months of training. The chances are that accidents will happen inside your house many times. Your puppy does not know right from wrong, and he cannot control his bladder or bowel. What is important is that you identify these situations and understand them. You need to learn to correct your puppy, so these mistakes do not always happen. This is the only way you can help him understand the training process.

Puppy parents will make mistakes when they try to handle accidents. However, you need to understand that puppies are not like human beings. They do not understand the concept of cause and effect. This is because the cause will always happen before the effect. It is not a good idea to punish your puppy when he has an accident. If he has had an accident a few minutes or hours ago, you cannot punish him after the act. This will only confuse him and will probably scare him. When you punish him after the act, it will create a strain on your bond.

Acting Without Overreacting to Accidents

Your reaction towards your puppy should always be within reason. You cannot have a severe reaction regardless of how badly your puppy messed the house. You should never engage in extreme punishments or punish him. Do not spank him or rub his nose in the mess. These punishments are only acts of cruelty. They will not help you raise your puppy in the right way. If you continue to do this, he will mistrust and fear you.

If you want to avoid accidents, you should always keep an eye on him. This has been mentioned earlier in the book. You should reprimand your puppy when you see him in the act. You should look for some signs to help you understand when your puppy needs to go. You must stop your puppy from relieving himself inside the house by using a command or sound. The minute you do this, take him outside. Take him to his spot and make sure he finishes relieving himself. Reward him after he is done. You must ensure that your puppy can associate going outside with a good response. It is your responsibility to keep an eye on your puppy. If you cannot do this for a long time, you should place him in a crate.

Prevent Remarking

You must clean up immediately after an accident. Since puppies have a strong sense of smell, they often return to the spot where they eliminated once. If you have not cleaned the place up, he can smell his urine, and he will walk up to that place. You cannot use only a detergent or soap, because that is not enough. If you want to remove the smell of urine or poop, you need to use a formulated stain remover, like Simple Green outdoor odor eliminator and similar products, to remove the smell from the floor. You need to have one at home before you bring him home. Make sure that you clean the area well. You also need to keep the puppy from that area, so he does not inhale the chemicals from the product.

Eight
Puppy Potty Training Mistakes

It is a tough job to potty train your puppy. Mistakes will happen even when you do everything in the right manner. Whether it is because there is some miscommunication between you and your puppy or from following wrong advice, it might seem like an unattainable dream to succeeding at potty training. In this chapter, we will look at some mistakes that puppy parents make. When you avoid making these mistakes, you will be a step closer to mastering potty training.

Skipping Crate Training

One of the most important pieces of equipment that you need to have at home for your training is a crate. If you cannot watch your puppy throughout the day, you can leave him inside the crate. This equipment will also make it easier to potty train him since you can tap into his need to keep his house clean. You can train him without using a crate, but the process will be longer. When you teach him to love his crate, you are creating a safe space for him. This will also improve his ability to hold onto his pee.

Lack of Supervision

Puppies can have accidents in a split second. It is for this reason that you need to keep an eye on your puppy during the training process. When you keep an eye on him, you can pick up on the signals and signs. You can then take him outside before he has an accident. If you cannot focus on your pup for the entire day or for a long time, you can use the crate.

Missing the Cues

Remember, puppies always display different types of behavior, especially when they need to go potty. Most puppy parents miss out on these hints, and this will lead to mistakes. Puppies have postures and signs that will say that they need to go. They may leave the room or act distracted. You need to recognize these signs and ensure that your puppy only goes outside. When you understand your puppy's body language, you know you need to take him outside immediately.

Forgetting to Praise

You need to praise your puppy verbally when he relieves himself in the correct spot. When he makes a good decision, you need to praise him. If you do not do this, it will slow your progress down because he knows that there is nothing for him if he is not praised. When you give your puppy a treat after he goes in the right place, he knows that he will get something in return if he goes in the right spot. This will make him want to pee or poop only in that spot.

Expecting too Much

Your puppy is learning slowly, and he has had a few clean days. You may assume that he is now going to do everything right, but you need to understand that there is a lot more that you need to do. You cannot expect your puppy to understand everything about potty training until he has had a few months with no accidents. You cannot slack off on the basics too soon because that will lead to accidents. You should continue to stick to the program until you are certain that your puppy understands you completely and that he only needs to go potty outside.

Not Understanding Hold Times

You must understand that it will take puppies time to control their bladder and bowel movements. You cannot expect your puppy to hold onto it for longer than they can because it is unfair. You can use the months-plus-one rule, but this will not apply to all puppies. Based on the age of the puppy, he may need to go every twenty minutes. If your puppy is sleeping, he can hold it in for longer than three hours. Regardless of the age of your puppy, you should take him out for a trip to relieve himself every few hours.

Not Treating Stains

Most puppy parents focus on the cosmetic aspect of accidents and worry about removing the stain from the carpet. When they fail to clean up the mess, their puppies will have more accidents in the same spot because it smells of urine. When you use water and soap or an ammonia-based cleaner that smells like urine, you cannot expect your puppy to stop going in the same spot. You should use a cleaner that will eliminate the odor and smell. We have looked at this in detail in the previous chapter.

No Potty Phrases

Yes, you can go out with your puppy and wait for him to go. You should try to use a phrase that will encourage him to go. You should teach him to go when you use a phrase. This trick will help you on a cold, rainy day or even when you are on a road trip. All you need to do is use the phrase multiple times in a day when he wants to go. You need to repeat this process twenty times a day. You can indicate to your puppy that he needs to get to business when you use the right phrase.

Using a Potty Pad

An absorbent potty pad is often sold as a training aid. However, these pads will prolong the process and also lead to some confusion. It is a good idea to use a potty spot inside your house instead of letting him make the entire house his toilet. The reality is that these pads will let your puppy know that he can go inside the house if he needs to. If you need to have a spot inside the house because of some logistics or health concerns, you can let him go inside the house. Use the same patch or pan that you use when you take him outside to pee or poop.

Using Punishment

This is one of the biggest mistakes that people make. You should never blame him for making a mistake inside the house. Remember, your puppy is still learning the rules of the house and the world. So, he is going to make a few mistakes. These mistakes are a reflection of your teaching. If you scold your puppy, intimidate him, rub his nose in the mess or scare him, he will be confused. He will be wary of even going outside because he is afraid of making a mistake. You need to use positive teaching techniques at all times. Remember, puppy training is a joint collaboration. You can ensure that your puppy understands the rules if you work together.

Frequently asked questions

When can I start housebreaking my puppy?

When you bring your puppy home, he is a part of your family. When he is a part of your family, he is old enough to be potty trained. If you wait for too long, your puppy will get in the habit of easing himself inside the house. He will be confused when you suddenly begin potty training. It is harder to break a bad habit when compared to building a good habit.

Can my puppy control himself for longer than eight hours if he can control himself for the night?

No. Your puppy can only hold it all night because he has not taken in any water or food during the night. He is not active. When he moves around during the day, walks around, takes a nap, eats, and drinks, he will need to relieve himself every few hours. As he grows older, he will have more control over his bowels and bladder, and he can go for longer periods without a break.

How often should I take my puppy outside?

You need to take him outside as many times as he needs. When your puppy is young, he will need to be taken out multiple times since he cannot control his bladder and bowel movements. If your puppy is less than six weeks old, you need to take him out every thirty minutes during the day. If he is between six and twelve weeks, you need to take him out every hour and so on. You can use the months-plus-one rule here, but it may not be accurate for every dog.

You need to take your puppy to his spot every time he comes out of the crate, rings the bell on the door, finishes playing, wakes up from a nap, or has eaten. Make sure to look for signs, and take him outside to relieve himself.

How do I handle my puppy if he wakes me up every night?

As puppies grow older, they will learn to make it through the night. This only happens when they are three months old. If your puppy cannot control himself even at that age, you can try to feed him earlier. You must understand that whatever goes in has to come out. You must tell your puppy that a midnight potty trip is not a fun trip. It should only be about him going potty and coming back. You should not play, give him treats, food, or water. You only need to walk out of the door to his spot and walk right back in. If he has too much fun in the middle of the night, he may want to do it every night, and you do not want that.

Can't my puppy learn from my older dog?

Yes, he can learn from your older dog, but this does not always work. A puppy will mimic an older dog, but you cannot know to what extent he will do this. Your training is what will instill good habits in your puppy.

Can I rub my dog's nose in it when he has accidents?

Do not do this! You must understand that your puppy will only associate correction when you catch them making a mistake. You cannot expect him to understand why he is being dragged to the puddle or pile after the act. This will only confuse him. If he has had an accident, you should only ignore your dog and clear the accident up. You can only correct his actions when you catch him peeing or pooping where he should not. If you find a lot of accidents but can never catch him in the act, you are not paying attention to your puppy. Remember, you must pay very close attention to your puppy. This is the only way you can reinforce good behavior. Think about it this way – your dog is uncomfortable. His bowel and bladders are full, and he knows he will feel relief when he empties on your carpet. Why should your dog go outside when it feels good for him to go inside or outside?

Conclusion

When you bring a puppy home, you must train him. This will make it easier to have a well-behaved dog at home. But the hardest form of training is potty training since a puppy does not have control over his bladder or bowels. So, you need to spend enough time training him, so he knows what he can and cannot do. This book sheds some light on how you can have a well-trained dog in seven days. If you stick to the tips and techniques mentioned in this book, your puppy will learn quickly.

Thank you for reading!

Printed in Great Britain
by Amazon